Nature's Yucky! 3

The Eastern United States

Lee Ann Landstrom AND Karen I. Shragg

ILLUSTRATED BY Rachel Rogge

Mountain Press Publishing Company
Missoula, Montana
2013

AUTHORS' NOTE

As longtime directors of nature centers, we strive to portray nature in a positive light. However, some things about nature can be gross, no matter what the reasons are for the actions. We hope that teaching children about the benefits of these yucky behaviors will give young people a greater understanding and appreciation of the amazing natural world.

Landstrom, Lee Ann, 1954–
 Nature's yucky! 3 : the Eastern United States / Lee Ann Landstrom and Karen I. Shragg ; illustrated by Rachel Rogge.
     pages cm
 Audience: Ages 5 & up.
 ISBN 978-0-87842-601-0 (pbk. : alk. paper)
 1. Animals—Food—Juvenile literature. 2. Eliminative behavior—Juvenile literature. [1. Animals—Habits and behavior.] I. Shragg, Karen, 1954– II. Rogge, Rachel, 1971– illustrator. III. Title. IV. Title: Nature's yucky! three.
 QL756.5.L37 2013
 591.5—dc23

                           2012051765

PRINTED IN HONG KONG BY MANTEC PRODUCTION COMPANY

Mountain Press
PUBLISHING COMPANY
P.O. Box 2399 • Missoula, MT 59806 • 406-728-1900
800-234-5308 • info@mtnpress.com
www.mountain-press.com

This book is dedicated to the family of Jody Trilling Shragg: Scott, Quinn, and Brooks—wishing you love and strength. —KS

To my husband, Jim. Thanks always for your support, love, and help —and for sharing nature with me. —LAL

For Finley and Penelope. —RR

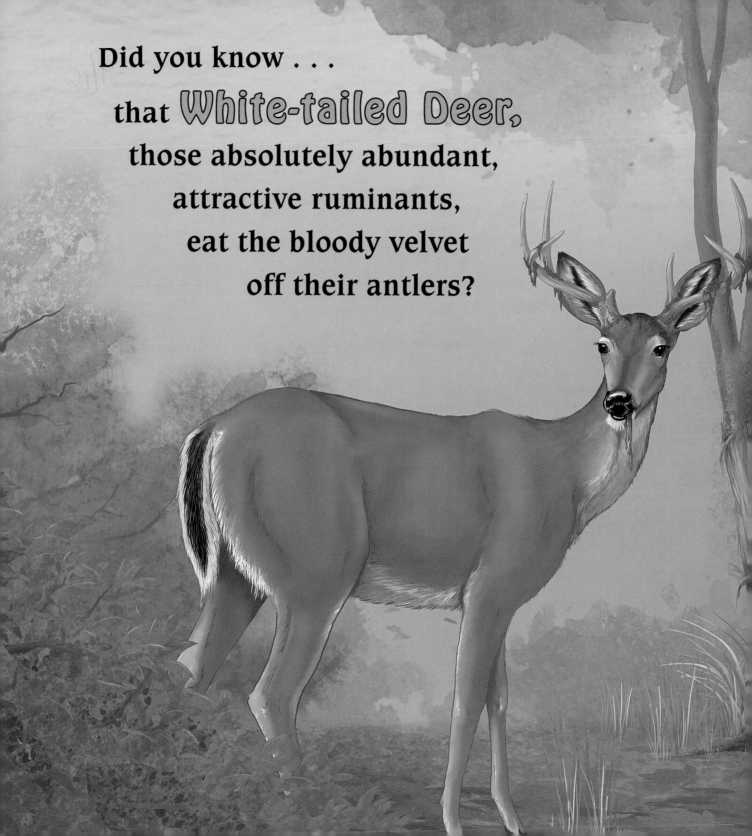

Did you know . . .

that White-tailed Deer,
those absolutely abundant,
attractive ruminants,
eat the bloody velvet
off their antlers?

Eeewww!! That's Yucky!

But hey, it's okay.
Just imagine if it weren't that way!

If it weren't that way, male deer, called bucks, would not get extra nutrition as winter approaches. Starting in spring, male white-tailed deer grow bony antlers, which are covered with a soft layer of skin, blood vessels, and fur called velvet. The velvet brings calcium and other nutrients to the antlers that helps them grow. The antlers stop growing in the fall, which causes the velvet to become dry and itchy. The bucks scratch and rub their antlers on small trees and eat the velvet as it falls off. Aren't you glad we just use velvet for fancy dresses and pillows?

Did you know . . .
that **Black Widow Spiders,**
those shy and secretive,
web-weaving arthropods,
sometimes eat their
mates for lunch?

Eeewww!! That's Yucky!

**But hey, it's okay.
Just imagine if it weren't that way!**

If it weren't that way, these spiders would miss an easy meal. Soon after mating, females may eat their mates for the nutrition needed to lay as many as four hundred eggs. Like many spiders, the black widow has a venomous bite that paralyzes her insect prey. She uses that same bite to stop her mate in his tracks before he can get away. The well-named spider is called a widow because she becomes a widow when she kills her mate. Maybe that's why there are no spider dating services.

Did you know . . .
that **Bobcats,**
those puny tailed,
perfectly poised predators,
use their tongues as
toilet paper?

Eeewww!! That's Yucky!

But hey, it's okay.
Just imagine if it weren't that way!

If it weren't that way, bobcats couldn't keep themselves clean. Without washcloths or toilet paper, these limber felines use what is available: their tongues! When kittens are really tiny, their mom licks their butts to make them go to the bathroom. Fortunately, licking their own rear ends doesn't make them sick. You can see house cats doing the same thing for the same reason. Makes you think twice about letting a cat lick your face to greet you, doesn't it?

Did you know . . .

that **Giant Swallowtail Butterflies,**
those fabulous, flittering, fluttering flyers,
look like bird poop when they are caterpillars?

Eeewww!!
That's
Yucky!

But hey, it's okay.
Just imagine if it weren't that way!

If it weren't that way, caterpillars wouldn't have much protection from all of the animals that consider them food. Disguised with blotchy markings that look like bird poop, the caterpillars go about their business of eating leaves. Their camouflage keeps them safe from birds, insects, frogs, and other predators. Often called bird-poop caterpillars, only the ones who don't become a meal may eventually turn into butterflies. Looking like bird poop is a great way to survive. Better to be disguised as something yucky than be on someone's menu.

Did you know . . .

that **Ant Lions,**

those secretive, sedentary, sinister doodlebugs,

can't poop at all when they are larvae?

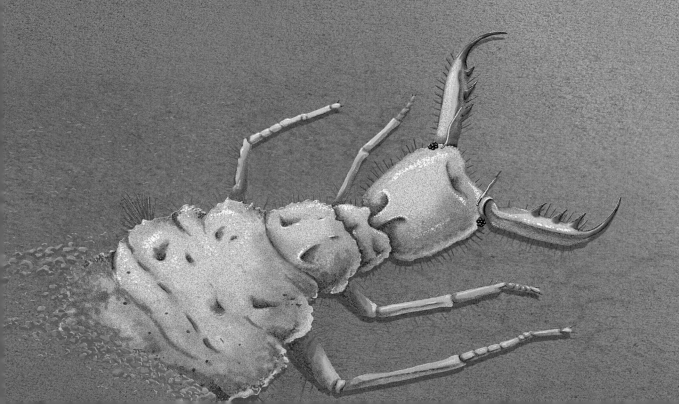

Eeewww!! That's Yucky!

But hey, it's okay.
Just imagine if it weren't that way!

If it weren't that way, ant lions would lose badly needed water. Young ant lions, called larvae, bury themselves in soft, dry sand. When most insect larvae poop, they lose some body fluid. To keep their bodies from drying out in their very dry burrows, ant lion larvae don't poop. Of course, as soon as they become adults, pooping is the first thing they do. Dirty diapers don't seem so bad now, do they?

Did you know . . .
   that **Walking Sticks,**
      those cunningly
         camouflaged,
            creeping insects,
               shoot a blinding, sticky
                  spray at predators?

Eeewww!! That's Yucky!

But hey, it's okay.
Just imagine if it weren't that way!

If it weren't that way, walking sticks might become easy meals for predators. These insects, also called two-striped walking sticks, have unique camouflage that makes them look like a small twig. If ants, beetles, mice, or birds do see them, walking sticks have another way to avoid being munched: they shoot a stinky white spray from their midsection, or thorax. Just like that of skunks, the spray of walking sticks temporarily stings and irritates their enemy's eyes, nose, and mouth. If walking sticks are on your menu, you might want to wear sunglasses and nose plugs.

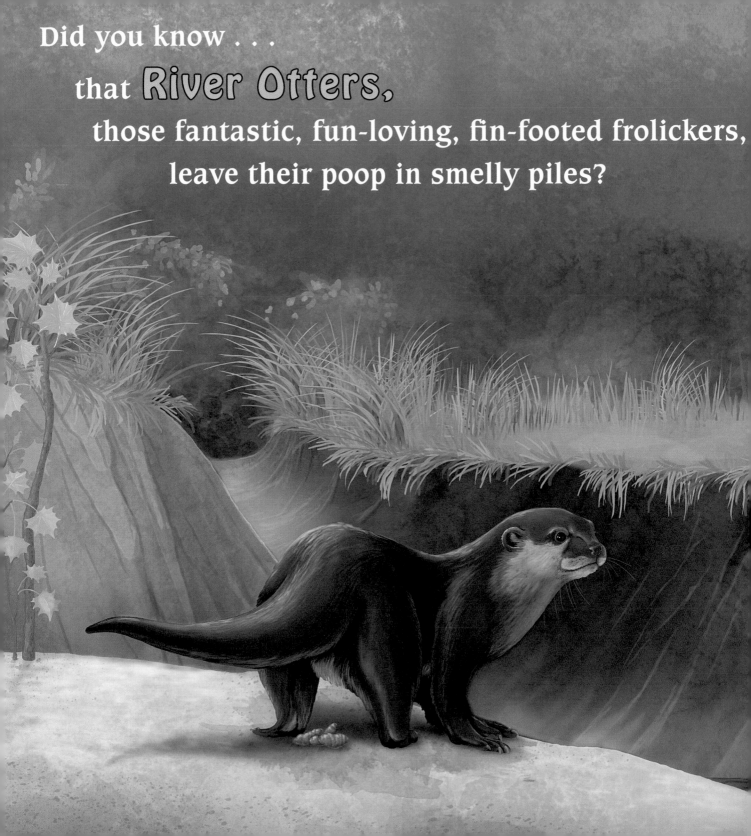

Did you know . . .

that **River Otters,**

those fantastic, fun-loving, fin-footed frolickers,

leave their poop in smelly piles?

Eeewww!! That's Yucky!

But hey, it's okay.
Just imagine if it weren't that way!

If it weren't that way, these playful mammals might fight over whose space is whose. Otters, like many animals, live in a particular area called a territory. River otters live in rivers and large streams. They leave stinky poop piles along the riverbank to tell other otters that this is where they live. If too many otters lived in one territory, they might eat up all the food and start fighting over what is left. By spreading out and not fighting, more otters can survive. Poop piles work well for otters, but aren't you glad fences were invented?

Did you know . . .
that **Dragonfly** larvae, those unusual, underrated, underwater insects, escape their enemies by shooting water out their butts?

Eeewww!! That's Yucky!

But hey, it's okay.
Just imagine if it weren't that way!

If it weren't that way, dragonfly larvae wouldn't be able to escape their enemies. These larvae eat small bugs, minnows, and even tadpoles but must watch out for larger bugs, fish, turtles, and even ducks that consider them a tasty meal. By forcing water out of the gill opening in their butts, dragonfly larvae can jet-propel themselves in the water and make a quick getaway. Fast-swimming larvae live to become dragonflies. Aren't you glad you can use flippers to swim faster?

Did you know . . .

that **Opossums,**

those pointy nosed, pouched prowlers,

ooze a green, smelly liquid when afraid?

Eeewww!! That's

Yucky!

But hey, it's okay.
Just imagine if it weren't that way!

If it weren't that way, opossums would be attacked more often
by predators. Opossums cannot run very fast, so they need other
defenses. When attacked by foxes, dogs, bobcats, or raccoons,
opossums will hiss, growl, screech, show their teeth, and drool.
If the predator continues to attack, "possums" roll over, play
dead, and ooze a nasty smelling green liquid from their rear end.
Turning yourself into a bad-smelling snack is pretty yucky, but
being a smelly survivor is better than being eaten.

Did you know . . .

that **Leopard Frogs**,
those lively, long-legged leapers,
can turn their stomachs inside out?

Eeewww!!
That's Yucky!

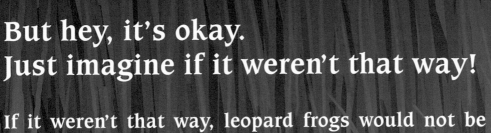

But hey, it's okay.
Just imagine if it weren't that way!

If it weren't that way, leopard frogs would not be able to get rid of a bad-tasting meal. This spotted amphibian empties its stomach by pushing the whole thing inside out through its mouth. The frog then wipes its stomach clean with its front legs before swallowing it back down. Its wide and soft esophagus, a tube-like structure going to its stomach, allows the stomach to pop all the way out of the frog's body. Aren't you glad your stomach stays inside when you eat something bad?

Did you know . . .

that Nighthawks,
those nimble, noisy, night flyers,
smell like stinky goats?

Eeewww!! That's Yucky!

But hey, it's okay.
Just imagine if it weren't that way!

If it weren't that way, nighthawks couldn't digest their favorite food: flying beetles. Hard beetle wings are tough to digest, but bacteria in the nighthawk's gut helps break down the beetle wings. This stew of bacterial gases smells nasty—like goats or stinky socks. If a nighthawk is caught or injured, it will poop right away. The bad-smelling poop may keep predators away. Isn't it odd that such graceful birds can smell so funky?

Did you know . . .

that Spotted Salamanders, those slinky, slippery "sallies," eat their own skin?

Eeewww!!
That's Yucky!

But hey, it's okay.
Just imagine if it weren't that way!

If it weren't that way, the salamanders would be wasting food.
Salamanders usually eat slugs, worms, crickets, and other little
creepy crawlers, but they also eat the skin they shed as they
grow. Frogs and toads, their amphibian cousins, do this as well.
This is a good example that in nature, nothing goes to waste.
Next time you have dry, flaky skin, be glad it's not your snack.

Did you know . . .

that **Brown Pelicans,**
those bag-billed, fish-catching, flawless flyers,
barf on their attackers?

Eeewww!!
That's
Yucky!

But hey, it's okay.
Just imagine if it weren't that way!

If it weren't that way, young pelicans could become someone else's dinner. Pelicans eat fish. If they are afraid, they barf up half-digested fish. Pelican chicks aren't able to fly until they are seventy-five days old, so until then, vomiting on attackers helps keep them alive. Can you imagine how bad they must smell?

Did you know . . .
that Red-spotted Purples,
those dainty, dashing, daring butterflies,
eat poop and drink pee?

Eeewww!!
That's
Yucky!

But hey, it's okay.
Just imagine if it weren't that way!

If it weren't that way, male butterflies would not be as good at attracting females. Males make smells called pheromones so females can find them. It turns out that the pee and poop of other animals is very high in nutrients, such as nitrogen, salts, unused sugars, and acids, which the butterflies need to make pheromones. Aren't you glad that perfume isn't made from urine?

Did you know . . .

that **Northern Fulmar** chicks, those gloriously graceful, gull-like seabirds, spit out sticky vomit at their predators?

Eeewww!! That's Yucky!

But hey, it's okay.
Just imagine if it weren't that way!

If it weren't that way, baby fulmars would be eaten more often by large hawks, gulls, and other predators. Fulmars nest along ocean cliffs in the far north. Young fulmars can't fly and have only one way to avoid being some other bird's breakfast: they spew out a sticky mixture of stomach oils and digestive fluids at their enemies. If an attacker is hit with enough vomit, it cannot fly and will fall into the ocean. Isn't it nice that fulmars aren't mad at you?

Did you know . . .

that **American Toads,**
those homely, husky, hiding hoppers,
pee in their predators' mouths?

Eeewww!!
That's
Yucky!

But hey, it's okay.
Just imagine if it weren't that way!

If it weren't that way, toads might get eaten more often. Toads have short legs and can't hop very fast. Predators such as foxes, dogs, or hognose snakes can catch them easily. If a toad can't get away, it will do many things to keep from being swallowed. It will pee, puff itself up to look bigger, and curl its head down and hunch its back. It also oozes a nasty tasting juice from its warty bumps. Only the hungriest of predators will eat a toad. After all, who wants a mouthful of pee?

More Fun Facts About Nature's Yucky! Animals of the Eastern United States

WHITE-TAILED DEER *Odocoileus virginianus*

Size: 37 to 87 inches (95 to 220 centimeters) long, including the tail, and 21 to 47 inches (50 to 120 centimeters) tall at the shoulder; males weigh 130 to 290 pounds (60 to 130 kilograms) and females 90 to 200 pounds (40 to 90 kilograms)

Food: green plants in the spring and summer; corn, acorns, and other nuts in the fall; and buds and twigs of many woody plants in the winter

Range: southern Canada and most of the United States, except for the Southwest, Alaska, and Hawaii

Antlers are living tissue and are among the fastest-growing tissues in the animal kingdom. The increasing amount of daylight in the spring stimulates antlers to grow. Bucks that are born blind cannot grow antlers because their eyes do not see the light, so their brains don't tell the antlers to grow. Antlers are useful for fighting between bucks. Once in a while, two bucks will lock antlers together and are unable to get untangled, resulting in their deaths. Antlers drop off in early winter, long after the rutting (mating) season is over. Mice and chipmunks gnaw on them for added calcium in their diet. Since white-tailed deer are very adaptable to disturbed areas where humans live, they are expanding their range and have overpopulated some areas.

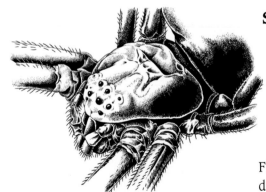

SOUTHERN BLACK WIDOW SPIDER
Latrodectus mactans

Size: females are 0.5 inch (8 to 13 millimeters) long with legs spread out and 1 to 1.5 inches (25 to 35 millimeters) in diameter; males are half the size of the female

Food: insects

Range: the southeastern United States, ranging from New York to Florida, and west to Oklahoma, Texas, and the Arizona and Nevada deserts

Though the black widow spider is the most venomous spider in the United States, people rarely die from their bites since the amount of venom injected is so small. Only adult females are dangerously venomous. They are shy and secretive and live in woodpiles, outhouses, and other undisturbed places. This infamous spider is sometimes referred to as the hourglass spider because of the red triangle markings on its belly that together look like an hourglass. Black widows puncture their insect prey with fangs and pump them full of liquids that turn the prey bodies into a soupy food. The widows then suck up the fluid. Black widows do have enemies. They are a favorite meal of the mud dauber wasp and praying mantis. The bright red markings, however, warn birds of their poisons.

BOBCAT *Lynx rufus*

Size: 19 to 49 inches (47 to 125 centimeters) long; males weigh 14 to 40 pounds (6 to 18 kilograms) and females 9 to 34 pounds (4 to 15 kilograms); adults stand 12 to 24 inches (30 to 60 centimeters) at the shoulders

Food: rabbits and hares; also known to eat rodents, birds, bats, fish, insects, and even adult deer, as well as lambs, poultry, and young pigs

Range: throughout the continental United States, southern Canada, and northern Mexico

Most active at dusk and dawn, this secretive feline is the most common wildcat in the United States. The bobcat is named for its tail, which is short, or "bobbed." They are fierce hunters able to kill prey that is larger than themselves, but they do not attack humans. They can leap up to 10 feet (3 meters) to pounce on prey. Bobcats can run up to 30 miles per hour (48 kilometers per hour), but they usually walk slowly, putting their back feet in the same spots where their front feet stepped. This allows them to stalk prey quietly. They are solitary animals who roam 5 to 50 miles (8 to 80 kilometers). Females raise a litter of one to six kittens that remain with her for nine to twelve months. Bobcats can climb trees and even swim if necessary. Their populations are stable and even growing in many areas.

GIANT SWALLOWTAIL BUTTERFLY *Papalio cresphontes*

Size: wingspan of 4 to 6 inches (10 to 16 centimeters)

Food: adult butterflies sip nectar from many flowers

Range: from New England west to Minnesota and south to New Mexico, including all of the southeastern United States

This butterfly gets its name because it is one of the largest swallowtails. Adult females lay yellowish-green eggs one at a time on plants. The larval stage, which are commonly called caterpillars, hatch and feed on plant leaves, including prickly ash, hop, rue, and citrus trees. Orange growers call the caterpillars "orange dogs" because they are pests on orange trees. Besides their shape and color, which make them look like unappetizing bird poop, the caterpillars have another way of defending themselves: they display a pair of orange, hornlike glands that emit a nasty smell. However, this second form of defense only works with predators that can smell.

ANT LION *Myrmeleon* species

Size: fully developed larvae are as long as a human fingernail, about 0.5 inch (13 millimeters); adults are approximately 1.5 inches (38 millimeters) long with a wingspan of 3.25 inches (83 millimeters)

Food: ants and other insects

Range: throughout the continental United States; also British Columbia and Hawaii

Ant lions get their name because as larvae they hide and wait to attack prey. Like butterflies, ant lions go through major life changes, a process called metamorphosis. After hatching from its egg, the larva looks for a place to dig a pit. It moves across the surface of the sand with backward movements, leaving artistic patterns that have earned it the nickname doodlebug. Ants and other bugs fall into the pits, and the ant lion quickly grabs them with its large jaws. When it is ready, the ant lion larva builds a cocoon that looks like rabbit poop covered with sand. An adult ant lion emerges from its cocoon having changed from a fierce-looking larva to an adult resembling a delicate damselfly.

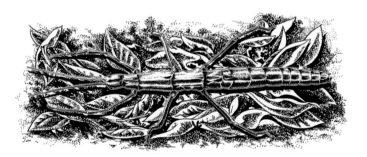

FLORIDA TWO-STRIPED WALKING STICK
Anisomorpha buprestoides

Size: females average 2.5 inches (64 millimeters) in length; males are smaller and more slender, averaging 1.5 inches (38 millimeters) in length

Food: leaves of a wide variety of trees and shrubs

Range: southeastern United States

This well-camouflaged insect goes by several other fun names, including devil's riding horse, prairie alligator, stick bug, witch's horse, devil's darning needle, scorpion, and musk mare. The last name comes from its habit of spraying a smelly spray to scare predators. The spray is produced and stored in two sac-like glands just behind the walking stick's head. The stinky ingredient in the spray is similar to catnip. Walking sticks are closely related to grasshoppers, crickets, mantids, and cockroaches. In the fall, females lay their eggs on or in the ground. When the immature bugs, called nymphs, hatch, they are green; they do not look like twigs until they mature. The walking stick is one of the few insects that can regrow its legs after losing them.

NORTHERN RIVER OTTER *Lontra canadensis,* formerly *Lutra canadensis*

Size: 26 to 30 inches (66 to 76 centimeters) long, with tail, 12 to 17 inches (30 to 43 centimeters) long; weight is 11 to 31 pounds (5 to 14 kilograms), males average 25 pounds (11 kilograms), females 18 pounds (8 kilograms)

Food: mainly fish, but also frogs, crayfish, tadpoles, and salamanders

Range: throughout North America except in the Desert Southwest and some Midwestern states

Otters are aquatic, which means they live in water. They have webbing between their toes on all four feet that helps them swim. They live in family groups in rivers, streams, wetlands, saltwater marshes, and beaches. Their home is a burrow tunneled into a bank or under fallen logs, with the entrance below water level. They also live in old muskrat huts or beaver lodges. Otters are famous for their playfulness. They play with their food, chase each other and wrestle, and love to slide down muddy or icy banks. They are in the weasel family, with minks, martens, ferrets, and skunks. The number of otters is decreasing because of trapping, accidental catching in fishnets, and pollution.

GREEN DARNER DRAGONFLY *Anax junius*

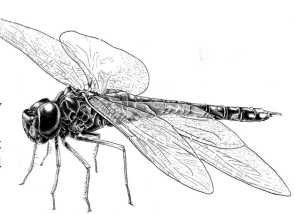

Size: 2.25 to 3.5 inches (57 to 89 millimeters) long with a wingspan of up to 4.5 inches (114 millimeters)

Food: adult dragonflies eat small flying insects, particularly midges and mosquitoes, but will also eat butterflies, moths, and smaller dragonflies; the larvae, which live in water, eat almost anything living that is smaller than themselves, and larger larvae are known to catch and eat small fish

Range: southern Canada south to Texas, Florida, and Mexico

Green darners are one of the largest dragonflies. They are dimorphic, which means males and females look different. Both sexes have a green thorax, which is the middle section of their body; however, males have a blue abdomen, which is the long back part of their body, while females have a purplish-gray abdomen. An adult's six legs serve as nets that catch and hold prey in the air. Like monarch butterflies, the northern population of darners migrates south as far as Texas and Mexico. Dragonflies can fly up to 85 miles (137 kilometers) in one day. The green darner is the official state insect of Washington.

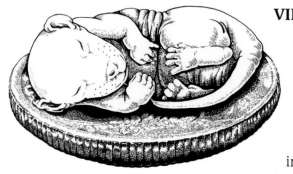

VIRGINIA OPOSSUM *Didelphis virginiana*

Size: 15 to 20 inches (38 to 51 centimeters) long with a tail that is 9 to 10 inches (23 to 25 centimeters) long; weight is 9 to 13 pounds (4 to 6 kilograms)

Food: insects, wild fruit and berries, dead animals, mice, frogs, and eggs

Range: the Southeast to Texas, and all of Central America; in recent decades, the Midwest, Northeast, and Toronto; has been introduced into parts of the West Coast, Rocky Mountains, and Southwest

American opossums are marsupials, a very old type of mammal. Marsupial mothers have pouches, and the babies are born at an age of twelve to thirteen days, before they are fully developed. When the eight or nine babies are born, they are the size of a dime and barely have arms. They crawl into their mother's pouch and stay there for two months, until their eyes open, their fur has grown, and they can walk. These kangaroo relatives are found in forests, farmland, and even suburbs. They live in holes, tree cavities, drains, culverts, hollow logs, and brush piles. These cat-sized mammals have fifty teeth, more than any other American mammal. They have thumb-like toes on their hind feet to help them climb trees. Baby opossums can grab a branch and hang by their tail. Opossums have been expanding their range north into the cold snowy states.

SOUTHERN LEOPARD FROG *Rana sphenocephala*

Size: medium-sized frogs up to 3.5 inches (89 millimeters) long

Food: green algae as tadpoles and a wide variety of insects as adults

Range: throughout the eastern United States, from New Jersey as far west as Nebraska and Oklahoma and south into the eastern third of Texas

Southern leopard frogs live near water in moist ground and vegetation; they escape predators by jumping into water. They are primarily nocturnal, which means active at night, and hide during the day in vegetation at the water's edge. Once abundant in North America, their population has declined in recent years because of pollution and deforestation spurred by urban growth, and because they're being collected a lot. Leopard frogs have smooth, moist skin that is highly sensitive to chemical pollutants in both air and water. Because of this, scientists pay attention to whether or not the frogs live in certain areas; if they don't, it can indicate that the area is polluted. For a long time students have used leopard frogs in biology class experiments, but because most of these frogs are caught in the wild, there is a movement to ban their use due to their declining numbers.

COMMON NIGHTHAWK *Chordeiles minor*

Size: 8.5 to 10 inches (22 to 26 centimeters) long with a wingspan of 21 to 24 inches (53 to 61 centimeters); average weight is 2.75 ounces (80 grams)

Food: mostly beetles, but also moths, flies, grasshoppers, and mosquitoes

Range: throughout the continental United States and southern Canada

Nighthawks were given their name because they swiftly hunt insects at night in forest openings, plains, suburbs, and cities. Like whippoorwills, they are in the goatsucker family, so named because people mistakenly used to think that the birds drank milk from goats with their very wide mouths. Nighthawks make nests on the ground or on flat, gravel roofs. Their feather patterns and colors camouflage them well. Nighthawk populations have decreased a lot, perhaps due to lack of nesting habitat, accidental poisoning, or fewer insects for them to eat due to pesticide spraying.

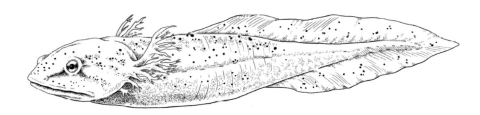

SPOTTED SALAMANDER *Ambystoma maculatum*

Size: 6 to 10 inches (15 to 25 centimeters) long; weight is 4.5 ounces (126 grams)

Food: crickets, worms, insects, spiders, slugs, and millipedes

Range: Nova Scotia west to Lake Superior, and south to Georgia and Texas

Though they are often mistaken for lizards, unlike lizards salamanders have soft, moist skin covering their long bodies and even longer tails. Salamanders also have four toes on their front feet, instead of the five that lizards have. They don't have scales, claws, or ears. They lay their eggs, which are surrounded by clear jelly, in water. Salamander larvae are sometimes confused with frog tadpoles, but their heads are not as large, and they have feathery external gills, while frog tadpoles do not. Spotted "sallies" are the state amphibian of South Carolina. Salamanders used to be more plentiful, but because they are sensitive to pollution and ultraviolet sunlight, and because they have lost so much wild habitat to human uses, they have become harder and harder to find.

BROWN PELICAN *Pelecanus occidentalis*

Size: 42 to 54 inches (107 to 137 centimeters) long, including the tail, with a wingspan of 6.5 to 7.5 feet (198 to 229 centimeters); bill is 11 to 14 inches (28 to 35 centimeters) long; average weight is 8 pounds (3.6 kilograms)

Food: many kinds of fish; sometimes shrimp and squid

Range: all along the Atlantic, Gulf of Mexico, and Pacific coasts

Brown pelicans were nearly extinct in 1962 because their eggshells were thinning and breaking due to use of the pesticide DDT. Now protected by laws, their populations have greatly increased. Pelicans live in flocks. They fly and glide in a single-file line and dive into the ocean at the same time with their beaks held open to catch fish. They are known for the large pouch under their lower beak, which can hold 3 gallons (11.4 liters) of water. They use their pouch to scoop up fish, like a net made of skin. Water strains out of the pouch at the edges of the beak, leaving the fish trapped. Pelicans don't carry fish in the pouch, though. They swallow the fish and carry them in their stomach back to their babies. Pelicans nest in trees and bushes, and sometimes on the ground. This state bird of Louisiana can live twenty-five to thirty-five years.

RED-SPOTTED PURPLE BUTTERFLY *Limenitis arthemis astyanax*

Size: 3 to 4 inches (76 to 102 millimeters) across

Food: larvae eat wild cherry, aspen, poplar, willow, hawthorn, and apple leaves; adults eat tree sap, fruit, carrion, bird and mammal poop, urine, and decaying wood, but rarely flower nectar

Range: southern Minnesota south to eastern Texas, east to New Hampshire and south to mid-Florida

Red-spotted purples are dark in color with mostly blue markings. Their two front feet are very small and are used for tasting, not walking. The caterpillars crawl to the base of a leaf, curl the leaf into a tube, tie it closed with silk, tie the leaf to the twig with silk, and spend the winter inside. The caterpillars wake up in April, eat more, turn into pupae for one to two weeks, and finally hatch as adult butterflies.

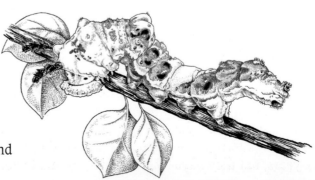

NORTHERN FULMARS *Fulmarus glacialis*

Size: 16 to 32 inches (41 to 81 centimeters) long with a wingspan of 40 to 44 inches (102 to 112 centimeters); average weight is 20 to 22 ounces (567 to 624 grams)

Food: shrimp, fish, squid, plankton, jellyfish, and carrion, as well as human food waste

Range: breed on the Aleutian Islands and along the coasts and islands of Alaska and the Canadian Arctic; spend winters at sea, in the Pacific Ocean south to California and in the Atlantic Ocean south to North Carolina

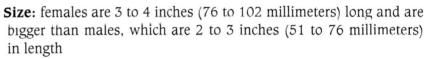

Fulmars come ashore only to breed; otherwise, they live out at sea. They nest on sea cliffs in groups called colonies. They do not start to breed until they are eight to twenty years old, which means they are slow to increase their population, thus they could easily become endangered. When nesting, the female lays one egg, which both parents keep safe and warm for about seven weeks, a period known as incubation. Once the egg hatches, both parents feed the chick with regurgitated fish, that is, puked-up fish. The northern fulmar is one of the longest-living birds. Several in Scotland lived to be at least forty years old.

AMERICAN TOAD *Bufo americanus*

Size: females are 3 to 4 inches (76 to 102 millimeters) long and are bigger than males, which are 2 to 3 inches (51 to 76 millimeters) in length

Food: includes earthworms, beetles, grasshoppers, spiders, slugs, algae, moths, ants, and tadpoles

Range: the eastern United States from Minnesota east to New England and south to eastern Oklahoma, Arkansas, northern Mississippi, northern Alabama, northern Georgia, and most of North Carolina; also found in southern Canada from eastern Manitoba to New Brunswick

Toads live near ponds, streams, wetlands, and lake edges and in meadows, forests, and even suburban backyards, orchards, and field edges. They hide during the day under logs, boards, flat stones, and woodpiles and may even dig a burrow or use mammal tunnels. Their bumpy skin does not cause warts on people; the bumps are just camouflage. The two biggest bumps, near their heads, hold bad-tasting liquid. Females lay jelly-like eggs in water; the eggs hatch into black tadpoles. The cold of winter causes toads to enter a state of inactivity, known as torpor, by burrowing, butt-first, several feet deep into the ground. Toad enemies include hognose and garter snakes, raccoons, skunks, ducks, owls, and opossums. In nature, toads may live five to ten years, but they have lived thirty-five years in zoos!

Bird-Poop Caterpillar Pretzels

This tasty dessert will remind you that in nature looks can be deceiving. It's a great treat for birthday parties, too!

Ingredients
- One bag white baking chips
- One package jumbo-sized pretzels

Instructions
Melt the chips in a microwave oven; stir until creamy. They may also be melted in a pan; stir the chips so they don't burn. Dip half of each pretzel into the melted chips and let them cool on waxed paper or a ceramic dish.

> **Tip:** Melt only one-quarter of the bag of chips at a time as they go far.

We recommend that you buy organic ingredients whenever possible. This is another way to help wildlife, the soil, and you. Organic food products reduce the amount of pesticides and herbicides used on farmland, which ends up in water; therefore, by using organic ingredients, you are helping to protect wildlife from exposure to pesticides and herbicides.

Make a Fur Wildlife Journal

Supplies
- Blank journal with lined paper
  (can have a hard or soft cover)
- Enough fake fur of any desired color or pattern to cover both sides of the journal
- White glue

Instructions
On the back side of the fake fur fabric, trace an outline of the journal.

Cut two pieces. Glue the fake fur onto both the front and back covers of the journal. Let the glue dry.

Once dry, your wildlife fur journal is ready for you to fill it with your observations of nature. You can describe how plants and animals look, write poetry, make a list of the wildlife you see, or even press plants you'd like to identify between the journal's pages. Have fun, and love nature in all of its yuckiness.

Resources

WEBSITES

About Birds
http://www.allaboutbirds.org
The Cornell Laboratory of Ornithology. Information, images, and tools to help identify birds; videos; nest cams; frequently asked questions; research.

http://www.wildbirds.com
Tips for beginner and seasoned birders, identification information, and bird locations.

About Bugs
http://bugguide.net
Images and information to help with the identification of North American insects, spiders, and their relatives.

http://www.whatsthatbug.com/
What's That Bug? Information and user-contributed images that help with the identification of North American insects and their relatives.

http://www.xerces.org
The Xerxes Society. Information about insects and other invertebrates.

General Information
http://animaldiversity.ummz.umich.edu/site/
University of Michigan's Animal Diversity Web. Great information on thousands of species.

http://www.allaboutwildlife.com/
All About Wildlife. Great information about endangered species that is kid friendly.

http://www.enature.com
Identification of most U.S. animal and plant species; games; birdcalls; information about parks and refuges; ask an expert; and more.

Organizations that Protect Wildlife and Habitat
http://www.audubon.org, National Audubon Society
http://www.biologicaldiversity.org, Center for Biodiversity
http://www.iwla.org, Izaak Walton League
http://www.nature.org, Nature Conservancy
http://www.nwf.org, National Wildlife Federation

BOOKS FOR ADULTS

Conant, Roger, and Joseph T. Collins. 1998. *A Field Guide to Reptiles and Amphibians: Eastern and Central North America.* Peterson Field Guides. New York City: Houghton Mifflin Co.

Elbroch, Mark. 2003. *Mammal Tracks and Sign: A Guide to North American Species.* Mechanicsburg, PA: Stackpole Books.

Evans, Arthur V. 2008. *Field Guide to Insects and Spiders of North America.* National Wildlife Federation. New York City: Sterling Publishing Co.

Hazard, Evan B. 1982. *The Mammals of Minnesota*. Minneapolis: University of Minnesota Press.

Oldfield, Barney, and John Moriarty. 1994. *Amphibians and Reptiles Native to Minnesota*. Minneapolis: University of Minnesota Press.

Opler, Paul A. 1998. *A Field Guide to Eastern Butterflies*. Peterson Field Guides. Boston: Houghton Mifflin Co.

Terres, John K. 1980. *The Audubon Society Encyclopedia of North American Birds*. New York City: Alfred A. Knopf, Inc.

Tyning, Thomas F. 1990. *A Guide to Amphibians and Reptiles*. Stokes Nature Guides. Boston: Little, Brown, and Co.

JUVENILE NONFICTION

Allen, Judy, and Tudor Humphries. 2004. *Are You a Dragonfly?* Backyard Books. Boston: Kingfisher (Houghton Mifflin).

Becker, John E. 2002. *North American River Otters*. Returning Wildlife. San Diego, CA: KidHaven Press.

Berger, Melvin, and Gilda Berger. 2000. *Do All Spiders Spin Webs?* Scholastic Questions and Answers Series. New York City: Scholastic, Inc.

Bredeson, Carmen. 2009. *Fun Facts About Salamanders!* I Like Reptiles and Amphibians! Berkeley Heights, NJ: Enslow Publishers, Inc.

Burns, Diane L. 1997. *Frogs, Toads, and Turtles.* Take-Along Guide. Minnetonka, MN: NorthWord Press, Inc.

Chinery, Michael. 1991. *Butterfly: Life Story*. Mahwah, NJ: Troll Communications, LLC.

Cooper, Ann. 1996. *In the Forest*. Wild Wonder Series. Denver, CO: Denver Museum of Natural History.

Cussen, Sarah. 2005. *Those Peculiar Pelicans*. Those Amazing Animals. Sarasota, FL: Pineapple Press, Inc.

Goldish, Meish. 2010. *Warty Toads*. Amphibiana. New York City: Bearport Publishing Co.

Hodge, Deborah. 1996. *Wild Cats: Cougars, Bobcats, and Lynx*. Kids Can Press Wildlife Series. Tonawanda, NY: Kids Can Press, Ltd.

Hurtig, Jennifer. 2007. *Butterflies*. Backyard Animals. New York City: Weigl Publishers, Inc.

Jacobs, Lee. 2002. *Deer*. Wild America. Farmington Hills, MI: Blackbirch Press.

———. 2002. *Toads*. Wild America. Farmington Hills, MI: Blackbirch Press.

Macken, JoAnn. 2009. *Opossums*. Animals That Live in the Forest. Delran, NJ: Weekly Reader Early Learning Library.

Markle, Sandra. 2011. *Black Widows: Deadly Biters*. Arachnid World. Minneapolis, MN: Lerner Publications Co.

———. 2008. *Stick Insects: Masters of Defense*. Minneapolis, MN: Lerner Publications Co.

Maruska, Edward. 2007. *Salamanders*. New Nature Books. Chanhassen, MN: Child's World.

Mason, Adrienne. 2003. *Otters*. Kids Can Press Wildlife Series. Tonawanda, NY: Kids Can Press Ltd.

Merrick, Patrick. 2007. *Dragonflies*. New Nature Books. Chanhassen, MN: Child's World.

———. 2007. *Walkingsticks*. New Nature Books. Chanhassen, MN: Child's World.

Murray, Peter. 2003. *Black Widows*. Nature Books. Chanhassen, MN: Child's World.

Parker, Steve. 2011. *Pond and River*. DK Eyewitness Books. New York City: DK Publishing.

Pascoe, Elaine. 2004. *Ant Lions and Lacewings*. Nature Close-Up. Farmington Hills, MI: Blackbirch Press.

Patent, Dorothy Hinshaw. 2005. *White-Tailed Deer*. Early Bird Nature Books. Minneapolis, MN: Lerner Publications Co.

Swinburne, Stephen R. 2001. *Bobcat: North America's Cat*. Honesdale, PA: Caroline House (Boyds Mill Press, Inc.).

Tatham, Betty. 2002. *How Animals Shed Their Skin*. New York City: Franklin Watts Library (Scholastic, Inc.).

Tekiela, Stan, and Karen Shanberg. 1995. *Nature Smart: A Family Guide to Nature*. Cambridge, MN: Adventure Publications.

Webster, Christine. 2008. *Opossums*. Backyard Animal. New York City: Weigl Publishers, Inc.

Picture Books

Bowen, Betsy. 1998. *Tracks in the Wild*. Boston, MA: Houghton Mifflin.

Dahl, Michael. 2006. *Do Salamanders Spit?: A Book About How Animals Protect Themselves*. Animals All Around. Picture Window Books (Capstone).

Dewey, Jennifer. 1994. *Can You Find Me? A Book About Animal Camouflage*. New York City: Scholastic, Inc.

Ehlert, Lois. 2001. *Waiting for Wings*. New York City: Harcourt.

Fleming, Denise. 1991. *In the Tall, Tall Grass*. New York City: Henry Holt and Co.

Luenn, Nancy. 1994. *Squish! A Wetland Walk*. New York City: Atheneum Books (Simon and Schuster).

Mazer, Anne. 1994. *The Salamander Room*. New York City: Dragonfly Books (Alfred A. Knopf).

Pratt-Serafini, Kristin Joy. 2001. *Salamander Rain: A Lake and Pond Journal*. A Sharing Nature With Children Book. Nevada City, CA: Dawn Publications.

Ryder, Joanne. 2007. *Toad by the Road: A Year in the Life of These Amazing Amphibians*. New York City: Henry Holt and Co.

Stone, Lynn M. 2003. *North American Pelicans*. A Carolrhoda Nature Watch Book. Minneapolis, MN: Carolrhoda Books, Inc. (Lerner Publishing Group).

Thompson, Bill, III. 2012. *The Young Birder's Guide to Birds of Eastern North America*. Peterson Field Guides. Boston: Houghton Mifflin.

Woelflein, Luise. 1995. *Metamorphosis: 9 Animals that Change*. A Pop-Up Lift-the-Flap Book. New York City: Dutton Juvenile.

Both **Lee Ann Landstrom** (left) and **Karen I. Shragg** are longtime educators of children and adults. **Landstrom** directs the Eastman Nature Center for the Three Rivers Parks District in Osseo, Minnesota. She has a master's degree in biology, is past president of the Minnesota Association for Environmental Education, and served for many years on the board of the Minnesota Naturalist's Association. She continues to lead eco-trips to Costa Rica and enjoys gardening, biking, and bird watching.

   Shragg is the naturalist/manager of the Wood Lake Nature Center in Richfield, Minnesota. She has a master's degree in outdoor education and recreation and holds a doctorate in education. She is an active advisory board member for the nonprofit World Population Balance. She teaches a class entitled "So You Want to Write a Children's Book" for community education. She is also the author of *Lucy's Hero: Remembering Paul Wellstone* and *Grieving Outside the Box: Stories of Hope and Resilience*. The previous two *Nature's Yucky!* titles have won numerous awards, including the Southwest Book Award, Best Books Award, and NAI Media Award.

Rachel Rogge studied art and biology at Humboldt State University, where she also worked at the Natural History Museum. She holds a graduate certificate in science illustration from the science communication program at the University of California, Santa Cruz. She is currently a full-time illustrator, working mostly on art for educational books. This is her second children's book.